Foiled Again!

Also by W V Butler

Young Detective's Whodunit

W V Butler

Foiled Again!

A dozen villainous schemes – each with
at least one hidden flaw. Can you spot
why each villain is going to end up by
being 'foiled again'?

Illustrated by Steven Appleby

DRAGON

Dragon Books
Granada Publishing Ltd
8 Grafton Street, London W1X 3LA

Published by Dragon Books 1985

British Library Cataloguing in Publication Data

Butler, William Vivian
    Foiled again
    1. Puzzles—Juvenile literature
    I. Title
    793.73   GV1493

ISBN 0-583-30720-5

Printed and bound in Great Britain by
William Collins Sons & Co. Ltd, Glasgow

Set in Times

For
Mary
with all my love
Bill

Contents

Introduction

Ask any detective – and he'll tell you that there is no such thing as the perfect crime.

Even the cleverest villain's scheme, if you look at it carefully enough, will contain some mistake which could lead to his (or her) downfall – provided, of course, that the police were clever enough to spot it.

In this book you'll be meeting a dozen or more villains, each of them carrying out some particularly nasty plan. They come in all shapes and sizes – from a small boy out to dig up the prize from the school treasure hunt (*The Treasure Hunt Cheat*) to a being from Outer Space plotting to blow up the whole human race (*The Destroyer of Planet Earth*). The cast-list also contains a murderous monarch from the time of Queen Elizabeth (*The Dangerous Queen*), a schoolgirl who tries to haunt a hated teacher (*The Gliding Ghost*), a foreign spy with dark plans to trap a crack British agent (*The Taxi Trap*), an evil doctor with irresistible hypnotic powers (*The Nightmare Crime*) and a good few – or perhaps I should say a bad few – more.

Some of these villains are pretty smart. Some are just fairly smart. Some are not too bright at all. At one time, in fact, I was thinking of calling this The Silly Villains Book – but that wouldn't be fair to the evil masterminds also included.

But however brilliant or otherwise their sinister plans may be, they all have one thing in common. At some point in each of them, the villain has made a mistake – or more often, several mistakes – and he or she ends by being, in the words of the old Victorian melodramas, 'foiled again'.

At the end of each story, there are points which you can award yourself for spotting the flaws in the villain's plan: 10 points in each of the first four stories (which are very short, just to get you started) and 30 in each of the other eight, which are longer and a lot more complicated.

So there are 280 points to be won in all. Score over 100 and you're an EFS (Expert Flaw Spotter). Score over 150 and you're a MFS (Master Flaw Spotter). Score over 200 and you're a CFS (Champion Flaw Spotter). Score over 250 and you're an AFFS (Absolutely Flawless Flaw Spotter) and a menace to every villain in sight.

Happy foiling.

W.V.B

1

The Monster Mistake

The Frankenstein party, held at Big Al's on Hallowe'en Night – Saturday, October 31 – was the biggest freak-out that there had ever been on the tough side of town. Villains and gangsters came from all over the district – and everyone had been invited to wear an identical Frankenstein monster mask!

The party started at midnight and was still

going on at eight the next morning, by which time all the 'Frankenstein monsters' had had too much to drink, and were reeling about looking more like real monsters than ever.

That was when the four Stephano brothers had their bright idea. It was the eldest, Steve Stephano, who really thought of it.

'Hey, listen, boys. Don't you realize what a great situation we've got here? All the villains for miles around are right here, all dressed up in the same masks. They're all drunk and none of them are gonna be able to remember where they are or what they've been doing.

'So all we've gotta do is wait until 9.30 and then nip out and hold up a bank, *still wearing our Frankenstein masks*.

'The fuzz won't know whether they're coming or going, because they'll have to suspect every villain in town – and *none* of them will have any kind of an alibi!'

The other Stephanos were so excited that all the bolts in their necks started shaking.

'You're a genius, Steve – a real genius!' said one.

'Hey, it's nearly nine,' said another. 'Let's get out of here, grab our guns and a car, and head for the nearest bank.'

Sharp at 9.30 the four Stephanos, still wearing their masks (which were really complete rubber heads) drove up outside the local branch of the London and Southern Bank.

They rushed out on to the pavement brandishing their guns and hurried towards the entrance.

It wasn't until they got there that they realized that they had been foiled again.

And by that time it was too late. A passing police Panda car spotted them, and suddenly they were being chased all over town.

The other Stephanos were changing their minds about Steve. 'You ain't no genius. You're a stupid nit!' they shouted. Ten points if *you* can spot Steve's monster mistake.

2

The Treasure Hunt Cheat

Miss Frinton, the English teacher at Hayfield Middle School, was organizing a great treasure hunt as part of the annual school fete. The treasure – four gleaming £1 coins hidden in a round tobacco tin – was going to be buried somewhere in the school grounds. Entrants were to be given a starting clue, and would then find other clues hidden round the grounds. (One starting clue, for example, was 'We've made

sure things start with a swing'. The next clue was to be found under the seat of one of the swings in the school playground – and so on.)

But one boy in Miss Frinton's class – an eleven-year-old villain called Bertie Binns – thought he could win the treasure hunt before it started!

The afternoon before the hunt, Miss Frinton had entered the classroom with a gleam in her eyes. 'I've just buried the treasure ready for tomorrow!' she said. And then she scribbled something on the back of an envelope, and put it in her handbag. 'That's to remind me of the exact spot where I've buried it,' she said.

Bertie Binns couldn't take his eyes off that handbag from then onwards. And at the end of the lesson, it so happened that Miss Frinton went out of the classroom, leaving it behind.

Bertie picked it up and ran after her with it down a long glass corridor linking the class-rooms.

'How very kind of you, Bertie,' a surprised Miss Frinton said. Bertie didn't often do kind deeds. She didn't realise that he'd taken the envelope out of the handbag on the way.

Back at his desk, Bertie read what was written on that envelope over and over again.

'FROM DOOR IN GLASS CORRIDOR – 4 PACES NORTH, 5 WEST.'

Well, that should be easy enough to work out, Bertie thought. The glass corridor was just outside the classroom, and the door mentioned must be the one leading out into the playground. All he had to do was work out which way North was, and then draw himself a map.

By a bit of luck, the next lesson was taken by the Science teacher, Miss Molesworth, who was talking about some seeds they'd planted in pots on the classroom window sill.

'This isn't a good window sill for plants,' she said, 'because this side of the school faces North . . .'

She had told Bertie just what he'd wanted to know. He hurriedly scribbled a map . . .

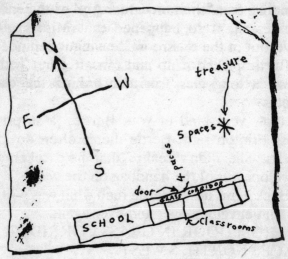

That night, when the school was closed, he crept into the grounds through a hole in the fence. He had brought with him a spade and a torch to read the map.

He made his way to the outside of the glass corridor door, had a quick look at the map by torchlight, and then started pacing.

He made each pace as wide as he possibly could, because he remembered that Miss Frinton was very tall, and had remarkably long legs. It wouldn't matter if he was a bit out, he told himself. He was prepared to dig a big hole.

In fact, he ended up by digging a very big one. But there was no sign of the treasure and all that turned up was the Head Teacher, who suddenly appeared and demanded to know what Bertie Binns was doing digging up his favourite flowerbed in the middle of the night.

Obviously, Bertie's plans have gone badly wrong somewhere. Ten points if you can say exactly where.

3

The Boy Who was Caught Red-Handed

David Greyfield wasn't really a villain, but he did once write a threatening note, intending to frighten the life out of his twin sister Cilla.

Cilla had been getting too big for her boots lately, and had refused to let him use the music centre which had been a joint present to both of them on their twelfth birthday the year before.

David reckoned that she was due for a scare. So he got a large red rubber washing-up glove, covered it with tomato ketchup to make it look nasty and gory, and put it in an envelope. Inside he intended to stick a note reading: 'The Red Hand will get you tonight.'

He realized, though, that he'd have to be very careful in writing that note. He had pretty weird handwriting, with very curly letters which Cilla would recognise at a glance.

For instance, this is how he usually wrote his name:

DAVID GREYFIELD

It was obvious that he'd have to write the note differently, with every letter thick and square, and not a giveaway curl in sight!

It wasn't easy. It took, in fact, more than an hour and a half of practice. But finally he managed this:

THE RED HAND WILL
GET YOU TONIGHT

'Cilla,' he told himself, 'won't recognise that in a million years.'

He wrote CILLA equally carefully on the outside of the envelope. Then he slipped out of the front door, popped the envelope through the letterbox slit, and gave a loud rat-tat-tat on the knocker – a very loud rat-tat-tat, because Cilla was in her bedroom, and had the music centre on at full blast!

He peered through the letter-slit as Cilla came down the stairs, picked up the envelope and opened it. He expected her to turn white and scream.

But all she said was:

'Come out, David, wherever you are. I can see you wrote this. I could tell it a mile off.'

Outside on the doorstep, David groaned and stamped his foot. He'd practised for an hour and a half. He hadn't written one letter in anything like his usual curly style. How could she possibly have seen at a glance that the note was his?

Ten points if you can say how David was caught – red-handed.

4

The Master Disguiser

By the time he finished, the Master Disguiser told himself, no one in the world would be able to tell him from Nero Kilberkoff, the richest man in London.

His disguise was always a masterwork!

With the help of a little flesh-coloured plasticine, he had given himself Kilberkoff's curious trumpet-shaped ears. His own hair and moustache happened to be very similar to Kilberkoff's, but both were black, whereas Kilberkoff's were grey. A little grey powder soon took care of that. Next he glued on two long grey sideboards, and fixed two grey eyebrows on top of his own. With infinite care, he clipped those eyebrows until they were, like Kilberkoff's, exact half circles.

Then, with the help of some more plasticine, he sculptured his nose into a precise copy of the long, thin Kilberkoff one. Tinted contact lenses gave his grey eyes the piercing Kilberkoff shade of blue. He had acquired a pair of spectacles exactly like Kilberkoff's, and was careful to

place them exactly where Kilberkoff did, three-quarters of the way down the nose.

He stood up and beamed at himself in the mirror. The disguise was perfect but, of course, a beam wouldn't do. Like most very rich people, Kilberkoff always looked cross, as though he'd just bitten on a very sour lemon.

The Master Disguiser carefully put on a 'sour lemon' look. Then he called out to his accomplices, in a close imitation of Kilberkoff's quavering voice:

'Hurry, gentlemen. We must be off to Lombard Street.'

Five minutes later, he was being driven to

Lombard Street in a luxurious Rolls. It stopped at the headquarters of the Metropolitan Bank. The manager was on the steps waiting to greet him, and didn't turn a hair when 'Mr Kilberkoff' asked him for a million pounds in notes.

'Of course, sir. But I'm afraid it will take us a little while to arrange. If you could call back at this time tomorrow, we shall have the money ready.'

The Master Disguiser didn't have to act to put on a sour expression. This meant that tomorrow morning, he would have to disguise himself all over again. And the Master Disguiser was an artist who hated to give a repeat performance . . .

A million pounds was a million pounds, though. So next morning, by now rather impatient, he went through the steps in the disguise routine once more.

First, he put on the trumpet ears. Then he dusted grey powder into his hair and moustache and glued on the grey sideboards. Next he worked for half an hour achieving the long, sharp nose; ten minutes putting on the half-circle eyebrows, and three minutes getting the spectacles at just the right angle.

Then he stared at himself in the mirror, frowning. He had an odd feeling that there was something he had forgotten. But he was already late for his appointment at the bank, and couldn't delay any longer.

So assuming the sour-lemon look and the quavering voice, he called his accomplices, and off they went to the Metropolitan bank.

The manager was standing just inside the doorway this time – and behind him were four cashiers, each holding a despatch-case containing a quarter of a million pounds in notes.

One glance at the Master Disguiser, though, and the manager started violently – and sent his cashiers away.

'Whoever you are,' he said sternly, 'you're not the gentleman who was here yesterday. Come into my office, please.'

The Master Disguiser did not accept this invitation. He turned and fled, his accomplices running beside him. And as the Rolls went speeding away down Lombard Street – the most elegant getaway car in the history of crime – he was still wondering desperately why he had been foiled again.

Ten points if *you* can say why.

5

The Perfect Theft

Ferdinand Mount was one of the cleverest jewel thieves in the world – and the theft of the famous Denton Diamond (worth over £500,000) from the Hon Mrs Sophie Denton was going to be the cleverest crime of his career.

That was what he told himself, anyway. And he had good reason for thinking he was right.

He had prepared the ground extremely carefully. Disguising himself as one Charles Bailey, the son of a millionaire businessman (who conveniently happened to be out of the country at the time), he had got himself introduced to Mrs Denton at a party, and they soon became friends.

After that, Ferdinand (or Charles, as he now called himself) frequently visited Mrs Denton at her luxury flat in Bruton Street, Mayfair; and before long, he was asking her to let him have a glimpse of her famous diamond.

'That's if it's not stored away in the vaults of some bank,' he said, with a grin.

'Of course it isn't,' Sophie Denton laughed. 'What's the use of having a beautiful stone if no one ever sees it except the vault-keepers, or whatever they're called? I always have the diamond right here.'

They were talking in her flat, in the room she called her 'study'. It was an odd room, as full of collector's pieces as a Bond Street antique shop.

Across one wall was a shelf, on which were arranged two flintlock pistols, two ivory elephants from India, a wooden giraffe (probably from Africa), a couple of bronze Siamese cats – and a large Chinese willow-pattern plate. The plate was at the back of the shelf, and Mrs Denton had to move the other objects to get at it. She put them carefully on the carpet beneath the shelf. Then she gingerly took down the plate revealing, behind it, the small circular door of a safe.

In the centre of this door was a knob, which obviously worked a combination lock. Ferdinand pretended to look away as Mrs Denton operated the knob, but out of the corners of his eyes, he noted exactly how many times she turned it. (Three times to the left, four to the right, seven to the left, then nine to the right.)

The safe door swung open with a click, and the next moment, Mrs Denton had taken out the famous diamond and was holding it in front of his eyes.

It was a huge stone – nearly 10 cms wide – and it shimmered and sparkled with all the colours of the rainbow – but coldly, like an Aurora Borealis trapped in ice.

'I'm sorry I can't let you hold it, Charles my dear,' Mrs Denton said. 'The insurance men are most particular that no one should actually touch it except me.'

Ferdinand beamed.

'It's enough of a thrill for me to *see* such a beautiful thing,' he said, although actually he was so anxious to get his hands on it that he could feel his fingers itching!

Mrs Denton put the stone back in the safe, closed the door, put the plate back in front of it and then rearranged the objects on the shelf in exactly the order they'd been in before.

'If ever I see these things in a different order,' she said, 'I shall know someone's been at the safe!'

'Very clever of you,' Ferdinand murmured, and hurriedly committed the order to memory.

'PEGECCP,' he told himself: pistol, elephant, giraffe, elephant, cat, cat, pistol.

He went away from the flat chortling. He had not only seen the stone, but knew now exactly where it was kept, and had even been shown the combination of the safe! There was something else, too. He had had a minature camera hidden in his breast pocket, and had taken a close-up snap in full colour of the magnificent stone.

29

As soon as the photograph was developed, he took it to one Wilberforce Lazaro, the most skilful forger of gems in London. In return for a little matter of £10,000, Lazaro made him a copy of the Denton Diamond ín paste – such a brilliant copy that only an expert could have told the difference.

Mrs Denton was always holding parties at her flat – and since Ferdinand (as 'her dear Charles') had become such a close friend of hers, he was naturally invited to the next one.

The party was held in the largest room in the flat, which Mrs Denton called the drawing room. The study was not being used that evening, and was dark and deserted. But Ferdinand tried the door, and found that it wasn't locked. All he had to do, he told himself, was wait until late in the evening, when most of the guests had had a lot to drink – and no one would notice if he slipped away for a couple of minutes. He reckoned that that would be quite enough time to take the diamond from the safe and slip the fake one in its place. If he didn't make any mistakes, it might be months before anyone realised that a robbery had taken place; and by then, it would be far too late for the police to work out when and how the stone had been taken, let alone by whom!

It was, in fact, nearly midnight when Ferdinand saw his opportunity. Mrs Denton rather prided herself on her singing voice, and was starting to give a selection of numbers from popular musicals, accompanied on the piano by a well-known composer. The piano was at the opposite end of the drawing room from the door that led into the study. As all the guests were crowding round Mrs Denton and her star pianist, no one so much as glanced round as Ferdinand slipped across the room and nipped through the study door.

The first thing he did was to close the door silently behind him. Next he clicked on the lights, and pulled out from his pocket the £10,000 fake Denton diamond. It was almost as

good as the original at shimmering with all the colours of the rainbow. But it didn't have quite the frosty grandeur of the real stone. It looked like an Aurora Borealis trapped in water rather than ice.

Ferdinand put the fake gingerly back in his pocket. Then he crossed to the shelf where the safe was hidden. Just in time, he remembered about fingerprints, and donned a pair of black leather gloves before touching any of the objects on the shelf.

One by one, he put the objects quietly down on the carpet. As quietly as he could, that is. The bronze Siamese cats fell against each other with a loud clink.

Fortunately at that moment Mrs Denton was practically raising the roof with an off-key rendering of *I Could Have Danced All Night*.

Above that, no one could have heard a bomb exploding, let alone of couple of cats clinking!

Wiping the sweat from his forehead, Ferdinand gently removed the willow-pattern plate, put it on the carpet beside one of the flintlock pistols and started to work the knobs on the safe. What was it now . . . three turns to the left, four to the right, seven to the left, then nine to the right . . .

The safe clicked open without trouble, and the next moment he had switched the two stones, and held the real Denton Diamond – all £500,000 worth of it – in his gloved hands!

Very, very carefully, he slipped it into his pocket – and had just clicked the safe shut when something terrifying happened.

Mrs Denton had finished wishing to dance all night; the guests had politely applauded, and the sounds outside had dropped to a babble of general talk. But two voices in that babble suddenly became very loud and distinct – and Ferdinand realized that it was a couple talking right outside the study door! What was more, they were obviously planning to come in. *The handle of the door slowly turned . . .*

Ferdinand acted faster than ever before in his long career as a thief. In a flash, he was over by the door, clicking off the lights. A split second later, he was removing the bulbs from the two lampstands that illumined the room.

The door opened. The light switch clicked.

'Oh, the lights must have fused,' a voice said. 'We'd better not go in. We might knock over one of Mrs D's collector's pieces.'

The door closed again, but the couple remained just outside, talking. Ferdinand replaced the bulbs, but didn't dare switch on the lights again. Fumbling in the dark, he picked up the ornaments one by one, and put them back on the shelf, taking care to keep to the order he'd memorized: PEGECCP, pistol, elephant, giraffe, elephant, cat, cat, pistol.

Then he crept silently across the room until he was just beside the door, and waited, his heart pounding. At last the couple moved away – and to his great relief, he heard the piano start again. Mrs Denton was giving an encore, which meant that everyone would be crowding at the other end of the drawing room, and his way was clear to leave.

Having committed what he believed was the perfect theft, he walked to the door and stepped out into the drawing room.

In fact, though, he'd made three very serious

blunders which between them made certain he'd soon be behind prison bars.

There's a total of 30 points if you can say what all three of them were, 10 points for each blunder.

6

The Destroyer of Planet Earth

Zavaldo arrived on Earth with his instructions from the Donyxian Council crystal clear.

The inhabitants of Donyx, a planet in a distant part of the galaxy, had been studying Earth for many years, monitoring all its radio and TV broadcasts. From these, they realized that human beings were pretty intelligent – almost as bright as Donyxians, and in some ways cleverer.

This made the Donyxians furious. They saw themselves as absolute rulers of the galaxy, but it looked as though one day the Earth people could take over that role . . . and it could happen in as little as 200 years from now, the Donyxian computers predicted.

The Council had therefore decided to remove all risk of that by destroying the Earth without delay.

They didn't possess the weapons to destroy it by bombardment from space. But if a small bomb made from their most powerful explosive, Donyxite, could be slipped into a crevice on Earth, and made to drop deep into the planet's crust, *that* should do the trick.

Zavaldo's mission, then, was a complicated

one. First he had to land his spaceship at night, in a quiet spot where no one would see it come down, as near as possible to the Hookey Caves in Cornwall, England. (A Donyxian planet-scan had shown that in the wall of one of these caves was a hole leading down to the deepest crevice on Earth – although the Earthmen themselves didn't know how deep it went.) Next, Zavaldo had to leave the spaceship, somehow find his way down to the caves, and slip the Donyxian bomb into the hole without any of the Earth people seeing what he was doing.

The bomb had a timing mechanism which, once set, would go off in an hour. During that time, Zavaldo had to get back to the spaceship and take off . . . leaving the Earth to explode into millions of pieces behind him!

The first part of Zavaldo's mission went off reasonably smoothly. He landed the spaceship (quite a small one – only about 5 × 10 metres) in a quiet wood without being noticed, but he found he had come down further from the Hookey Caves than he had intended – about 20 miles away instead of 2.

He could walk the distance, but thought it would be quicker if he took one of the Earth people's vehicles – called, he believed, cars.

From their close study of the Earth's TV programmes, the Donyxians knew all about cars and how they could be driven. Zavaldo had taken a course on the subject. He had also been specially trained to look and behave like an Earthman, and could even speak a little English. This was not terribly difficult. Apart from one big difference, which could be concealed if he took enough care, Donyxians looked exactly like human beings, although their eyes had rather a curious slant, and their skin was a little redder. Dressed in clothes carefully copied from the TV programmes, and with the Donyxian bomb hidden in a smart, Earth-style briefcase under his arm, Zavaldo believed he could easily pass as a human being, especially since it was dark. The Donyxian atmosphere was very similar to the Earth's, so he had no trouble breathing; and the gravity was almost exactly the same, so it wasn't hard to keep his balance.

Zavaldo had arrived at about 8 P.M. on a mild October evening – a time when there were plenty of cars about. As soon as he stepped out of the woods where he had landed his spaceship, he saw one of these strange Earth vehicles, 'cars', parked at the side of the road.

He walked over to it. The doors were locked, but he had a Donyxian metal-melting ray device with him, and that soon enabled him to burn through one of the locks. A moment later, he had climbed into the driving seat, and was leaning back behind the wheel. He didn't lean back for long. Earthmen's driving seats weren't built for Donyxians, and a sharp pain shot all down his back.

'*Zaroyshoof*!' muttered Zavaldo – a Donyxian phrase it is probably better not to translate.

He hurriedly leant forward and then, remembering what he had learnt on his Earth driving course, succeeded in starting the car.

No sooner had it moved away from the kerb, though, than another car pulled up alongside. A strange car, with a blue light on the top and a wailing siren. Its driver was wearing a uniform, and was shouting and waving at him.

Zavaldo realized that he was being stopped by a policeman. His blood ran hot – not cold, as an Earthman's would have done. He wondered if they'd spotted the hole near the door handle which his ray-gun had made.

'What – what is it please?' he asked hoarsely.

'Seat belt!' the policeman yelled. 'Fasten your seat belt. Don't you know it's the law?'

'Oh! Oh! Seat belt . . . Ah! So! Yes. Thank you,' Zavaldo spluttered. His accent sounded half Chinese and half Hungarian, with an animal grunt or two thrown in. Seat belts had not been mentioned on his course, but it wasn't hard to work out what was required. He picked up the belt and fastened it round him.

'Okay, huh?' he called.

The policeman nodded, and Zavaldo was allowed to drive away. He wasn't very comfortable, though. Like driving seats, these belts were definitely made for Earthmen, not Donyxians. Once again he felt that stabbing pain down his back.

He drew up outside the entrance to Hookey Caves at 9 P.M., just when they were closing to the public. Getting out of the car, he found himself in more trouble. Ahead of him were some revolving doors, something else that hadn't been mentioned during his Earth training. He whirled round and round in them for a good two

minutes before he could find a way to get out – and then, just as he was finally stepping clear, something caught. He heard a loud ripping noise and groaned. It felt as though his suit had split right down the back.

He was tempted to turn and run. But he was so close to carrying out his master-plan that he decided to carry on regardless.

He was now in a small hall. The entrance to the caves was straight ahead of him, but first he had to get past an attendant who was sitting at a small table alongside it.

Zavaldo strode right up to the table, smiled at the attendant, and tried to slide past sideways without letting the man see his back.

The attendant wasn't having any of that.

'Here! What are you playing at, matie? It costs £1 to go through there, and anyhow I'm afraid we're closing. Come back tomorrow – '

'I'm sorry,' said Zavaldo. 'I do not speak Earthlish – I mean English – too good.'

The attendant took a deep breath, and started to explain again.

'You need a ticket to get past here, matie, costing £1. And in any case, we're clos – Hey! Hey! What – '

Zavaldo had by now shot past him and, still smiling amiably, was backing towards the corridor that led to the caves.

'Hey!' yelled the attendant. 'Hey – come back! Oh, oh – my Gawsh – '

Zavaldo had suddenly turned his back. The attendant turned as white as a sheet, and his eyes were nearly popping out of his head. He was too stunned to give chase, but not too stunned to press an alarm bell beneath his table. Two policemen arrived in seconds.

The attendant could hardly speak, but he pointed in the direction Zavaldo had taken. The policemen rushed headlong down the corridor.

It was a long, winding corridor. By the time they had rounded a bend in it and spotted him,

Zavaldo was only a bare three metres away from the hole in the wall – that hole that led to a crevice running deep into the earth's crust.

He laughed – a hyena-like Donyxian laugh of triumph.

Two more strides and he'd be close enough to that hole to throw the briefcase down it, at the same time pressing the catch that started the timing mechanism. After that, nothing and nobody could stop the Donyxian Council's plan for the destruction of Planet Earth. The policemen were still a good three paces behind him – and neither of them had those strange Earth contraptions he'd heard about called 'guns'. So how could they stop him now?

'Earthmen,' roared Zavaldo, 'you are finished! You and your whole stupid planet! All of you are finished – for ever!'

And he started to make those two fateful strides. Before he'd finished the first of them, he was suddenly halted, dead in his tracks, and the corridor rang with a fearful Donyxian oath. *'Zaroyshorrrofoooo . . .'*

Try as he would, Zavaldo couldn't move – and he was suddenly in such agony that the briefcase dropped from his hands to fall harmlessly to the rocky floor, less than ten centimetres from the hole in the wall. Still cursing and swearing, Zavaldo pulled out a deadly Donyxian death-ray gun – but then he writhed in agony again, and that dropped from his fingers too.

'Whoever or whatever you are,' one of the policeman said coldly, 'I think you'd better come along with us.'

'That's right,' said the other.

The policemen were still a good three paces away. And neither of them had a gun, a knife, or any other kind of weapon. Yet Zavaldo knew that he was helpless, and all he could do was mutter under his breath '*Zakosheebashleeshi*.' Which happens to be Donyxian for 'Foiled again!'

Fifteen points if you can say what had happened to him – and fifteen more if you can spot the three clues hidden in the story.

7
The Gliding Ghost

All through the Autumn term at Benwick-on-Sea Middle School, the French mistress, Miss Frenais, had been getting into Celia Webster's hair. 'You are zee stupidest girl at French that I have evair taught – evair!' she said, and lesson after lesson she had made Celia the laughing-stock of Class 6B.

Celia, an eleven-year-old with short dark hair and very brown beady eyes, wasn't the sort to take that lying down. She didn't say much – she never did say much to anyone about anything – she thought a lot, and spent hours brooding about how she could get her revenge.

Then suddenly she had an idea – and funnily enough, it was Miss Frenais herself who suggested it. One day, getting on towards Hallowe'en, she told the class she was going to give them a ghost story in French to translate.

'But I am going to make it easy for you – even ze stupidest of you!' she said with her usual glare at Celia.

Miss Frenais had thick, square spectacles which made her eyes look twice as large as they

46

really were – and her glare twice as ferocious! 'I am going to give you ze story in English first,' she went on. 'It's a true story, which you may already know. Outside zis very school there are the ruins of an old monastery. It belonged to monks of a French order, and the abbot in charge of the monastery had a French name. He was known as – 'Celia couldn't quite catch the name but it sounded like 'the Abbé Huge', and she imagined a vast giant of a man towering over everyone at the monastery. She really wasn't very good at French, or she'd have noticed that Miss Frenais made a growling noise at the back of her throat when the pronounced the name, which is the French way of saying 'r'.

'Back in ze Middle Ages,' Miss Frenais went on, 'zere were more than a hundred monks in ze monastery. But one stormy night, *zut*! somezing happened – no one knows what – and next morning, zey were all gone. Some say ze place was hit by a plague and zey all died. Others say the Devil appeared, and zey all fled away back to France. At all events, no one has lived in ze monastery from zat day to zis. But evair since zen, people passing by the ruins at night 'ave reported seeing a robed, hooded figure gliding along on top of ze monastery wall. Zey say it is ze Abbé, perhaps still fleeing from ze Devil, perhaps weeping over his vanished monastery.' Miss Frenais's eyes were no longer glaring. They were suddenly wide with fear – and those square spectacles, which exaggerated everything, made them look wide with terror. 'Every Wednesday night, I take an evening class for adults in ze school building, which doesn't end until 'alf past nine. Afterwards, I have to walk 'ome past zose ruins. And I always cross myself as I do so – 'oping and praying that I don't see ze Abbé. Because ze story goes zat if you *do* see him – soon afterwards, you disappear forever, just like zose monks of long ago!'

Celia's eyes, for once, were looking more like slits than beads. There was nothing she would like better than for Miss Frenais to see the ghost

– and disappear forever. And she remembered that today was Wednesday, which meant that tonight, at 9.30, Miss Frenais would be taking her weekly walk right past those ruins! If only she could come up with a plan –

She started thinking furiously. The monastery ruins were so close to the school that she could see them from the classroom window. Not much of the ancient building was left after all those years: just a few arches with a long, low, tumble-down wall in front of them – the wall along which the ghost of the Abbé was supposed to glide.

Celia stared hard at the wall. It was only about two metres high, and it looked as though a smooth concrete path, built specially for sight-seers, ran behind it. She could tell that from the bits of the path showing on either side.

That was when she had her brainwave. Her parents were always out late on Wednesday nights, attending rehearsals for an amateur play, and they left her alone in the house. (She was too old these days, they reckoned, for a baby-sitter!) And her home was only a few minutes from the school. Supposing she sneaked out at 9 o'clock and came down to the ruins, and hid behind that wall? She could bring with her that old green winter coat she had, the one with a thick hood. If she folded the coat round a broom handle, and raised it above her head, it would come to just the right height above that wall to look like a ghost. And if she walked along behind the wall, and held it steadily, it might look as though it was gliding . . .

Suddenly a second brainwave hit her – this time such a brilliant one that it seemed to explode like a firework inside her head. Supposing she didn't just walk along the path – but *roller-skated*? Then the ghost would certainly seem to be gliding – fleeing from the Devil at the speed of light!

And she should be able to roller-skate really fast along that path. It looked as though it sloped sharply downwards in the middle. Just there, it would be almost like skating downhill . . .

Celia would have liked to have taken a closer look at those ruins. But some of the arches weren't too safe and the whole place was out of bounds to the pupils of the school – a rule that couldn't be disobeyed, since the spot was in full view of the Head Teacher's windows. It didn't matter anyway, she thought. She'd seen all she needed to see. The wall was quite tall enough to hide her from sight. The concrete path was perfect for roller-skating. And that old hooded coat, on the end of a broomstick, would show quite clearly over the top of the wall, if she held it right above her head. She decided that she'd tie a couple of pillows round the broomstick to pad the coat out and make it bulge. You couldn't have anything too skinny-looking for the ghost of the Abbé Huge . . .

Her master-plan was now complete. All she had to do was wait until tonight, when she could put it into action.

Celia was too excited to pay any more attention to the French lesson – or any other lesson – for the rest of the day. And when she got home, she was too excited to eat more than half a sausage and a few beans at suppertime. She rushed upstairs the moment her parents had gone, and spent what seemed like hours rigging up her effigy of the Abbé Huge. It took far longer than she'd thought it would. The coat kept coming off the broom handle, and the pillows refused to stay tied in place.

At last, though, she was ready, and at just ten minutes to nine she stepped out of the house. She already had her roller-skates on and, with the rigged-up 'ghost' under one arm and a torch firmly clutched in the other, streaked off down the road.

Almost immediately she hit trouble. Turning a corner too fast, she cannoned into a lamp-post, and her torch went flying. It fell on the pavement with a crash and a tinkle of broken glass,

and was obviously out for good. Not that that mattered. It was a clear, frosty night and the moon up above was shining with almost the force of a giant headlamp in the sky. She'd be able to see quite well enough for everything she had to do, she thought.

But even the brightest moons leave black shadows, she discovered when she finally reached the ruins. Once crouching behind the ancient wall, she found herself in pitch darkness, scarcely able to see the fingers on her own hands which were suddenly cold and shaky, and felt colder and shakier with every second that passed.

These old ruins hadn't looked very frightening in broad daylight, seen from the classroom window. But now, in the cold, eerie moonlight, those tumbled archways looked like something out of a horror movie. And under each arch were dense black patches of shadow that seemed to move as she stared at them. Anything could be hiding there, waiting to pounce, she told herself . . . perhaps even the ghost of the Abbé Huge himself!

With a great effort, Celia pulled herself together. Ghosts didn't *pounce*, she told herself severely. They *glided* . . . which reminded her, it was almost half-past –

She had no time to finish the thought. At that very moment she heard quick, tapping footsteps on the pavement the other side of the wall, and peeping over it, saw that Miss Frenais was just about to come past.

Taking a deep breath, she seized the broomstick effigy, raised it high above her head, and began to skate at high speed along the dark path.

At first, her Master Plan seemed to be succeeding magnificently. She heard a terrified gasp from the other side – as though Miss Frenais was just about to faint, or to start running for her life.

But Miss Frenais' terror didn't last for long.

Within a second, something happened which told her for certain that the apparition was only a schoolchild's stunt.

Shortly after that, something still worse happened, from Celia's point of view. Thinking it over, Miss Frenais realized that only one of the children she taught could have been responsible, and called out:

'It is *you*, isn't it, Celia Webster . . . you stupid, stupid child!'

Fifteen points if you can say what happened to show it was just a stunt. And you deserve fifteen more points if you're sharp enough to spot why Miss Frenais was so sure that it was Celia who was behind – or, rather, underneath – the Gliding Ghost.

8
The Taxi Trap

'Here are your orders,' barked the voice on the telephone, so loudly that the receiver seemed to jump up and down in Stefan Kraski's hand.

'At twelve noon precisely on Wednesday the 2nd,' the voice went on, just a shade more calmly, 'the British secret agent, Maurice Fayne, will be arriving at Buktaan Airport, in the Middle East, on the flight from London. He will be travelling under his own name, and won't be in disguise, so you will have no trouble recognising him. He is fair-haired, tall – 6ft 4in – with blue eyes and a curious, crooked smile. He has booked a room at the Prince Husaan Hotel, Buktaan, and will probably want to go straight there from the airport. It is your task to see that he never arrives at the hotel. Instead, you will bring him to me at our new Buktaan headquarters, either gagged, bound and blindfolded – or better still, completely unconscious. He must not see where our headquarters are – it is something British Intelligence would give a great deal to know.'

Stefan Kraski nodded, briskly. He was a

small, bald man with eyes that were always narrowed, as though he was constantly thinking up sinister schemes.

'This sounds to me like a case for the taxi trap,' he said. 'It is an old trick, but it rarely fails. If you could supply me with a car that looks exactly like one of the local Buktaan taxis, but has several rather special features – '

'You can have whatever equipment you need,' the voice replied. 'But be careful. Maurice Fayne is one of the most cunning and resourceful agents in the British secret service.'

Kraski laughed scornfully.

'You forget who you are talking to, Contact 33,' he said. ('Contact 33' was the only name by which he knew the owner of the voice on the phone.) 'I am one of the most cunning and resourceful agents in *any* secret service. Mr Maurice Fayne will certainly not escape *me*!'

He went on to describe the vehicle that he wanted in detail. From the outside, it would look just like a normal taxi. But once the driver pressed a secret button, it would become a very unusual taxi indeed. The doors would lock themselves. The glass panel between the passenger and the driver would slide shut, and be hermetically sealed. Any windows that were open would slide shut too.

Both windows and the panel would be made

of tough bullet-proof glass, so tough that it could not be broken by any kicks or punches. The doors and the walls would be of specially reinforced metal, too – proof against any weapons or instruments Maurice Fayne might have on him.

The taxi would have one other unusual feature. At the touch of a second button, from half a dozen pieces of steel piping hidden under the seats and other places round the inside, a special 'knock-out' gas would come pouring out. Within seconds, Maurice Fayne would not even be trying to escape from the taxi trap. He would be lying unconscious across the seat or on the floor . . .

Contact 33 grunted approvingly.

'That all sounds very satisfactory, Kraski. But there is just one possible flaw in your scheme. There will be a lot of taxis waiting at the airport. How can you be sure that Fayne will choose yours?'

'He is bound to,' Kraski told him. 'Mine will be the nearest and most comfortable-looking taxi there. I will make sure that it stops right alongside him the moment he comes out of customs.'

'But won't that make him suspicious?'

'No one is ever suspicious of Stefan Kraski,' Kraski said. 'Stop worrying, sir. Leave it to me.'

Secretly, though, Stefan was just a little worried himself. If this Fayne was as smart as everyone said, it might be more difficult than he'd supposed to get him into the taxi trap.

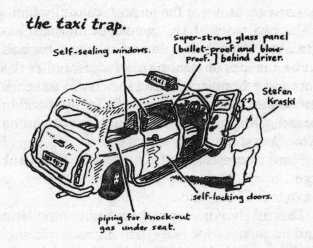

the taxi trap.

Self-sealing windows.

Super-strong glass panel [bullet-proof and blow-proof.] behind driver.

Stefan Kraski

TAXI

self-locking doors.

piping for knock-out gas under seat.

He decided not to take any more chances than he could help. He left for Buktaan straight away, and spent several days studying the way the taxi-drivers round the airport looked and talked.

On the morning of Wednesday the 2nd, he spent hours giving his face exactly the right Middle Eastern tan. Then he donned Arabian clothes and set out for the airport. On the way, he decided that the vehicle Contact 33 had supplied was too new-looking. It stood out a mile. He stopped beside the road, and threw sand and grit over it so that it would look only about twice, instead of ten times, as smart as the other taxis in the row.

Then he drove to the airport, carefully timing his arrival so that this would be the first taxi Maurice Fayne saw. It was a tense moment when the British agent finally appeared on the scene. As Contact 33 had predicted, Stefan had no trouble recognizing him. His fair hair and his height made him impossible to miss. And he was smiling that famous crooked smile.

'Taxi, meester?' said Kraski, in a thick Buktaan accent. 'Me get you to hotel queeek as flash.'

Maurice Fayne's crooked smile broadened and became a wide, silly sort of grin.

'Just what I want,' he said. 'I *am* in a bit of a hurry. Prince Husaan Hotel, please. Fast as you can.' He showed no signs of being suspicious – or of having any brains in his head at all.

As the greatly-relieved Kraski loaded his luggage in the boot, Fayne made one of the stupidest remarks the foreign agent had ever heard. 'Not bad weather for the time of year,' he said – as if it wasn't as hot as this at Buktaan almost every day from January to December!

Hiding his contempt, Stefan simply murmured: 'Ah, yes, meester. Very good weather today. Hop in now, please, and I get you to hotel double-quick.'

'Right. Thanks very much,' said Fayne, his grin stupider than ever. Then he jumped into the rear of the taxi, slamming the door behind him.

Stefan felt like shouting aloud with triumph as he climbed in the front behind the wheel. All his worries were over. The oh-so-clever British agent had cheerfully walked right into the trap, and slammed the door behind him! Nothing on earth could stop his plan succeeding now . . .

As he started the engine, and drove away from the airport, Stefan pressed the first of the two secret buttons. Immediately the glass panel slid shut behind him, and all the open windows

61

in the rear of the car closed. Obviously Maurice Fayne realised he was trapped. Stefan could hear him banging his fists helplessly against one of the doors. The blows sounded very faint, obviously because of the thickness of the partition.

Stefan switched on a microphone, which meant that every word he said could be heard plainly at the back of the car.

'It is no use, Mr Fayne. You cannot punch your way out of this trap. No!' he added with a mocking laugh, as the sound of a revolver shot crashed out. 'You cannot shoot your way out of it, either. The doors and the glass will resist all blows *and* bullets!'

He could hear faint shouts now – Fayne was yelling: 'Stop the car!' and 'Let me out at once!' Almost as stupid as his remarks about the weather, Stefan thought. If this was the cleverest agent in British Intelligence, than surely Britain was in a pretty desperate state. He laughed still more mockingly. He was not afraid that anyone would hear the shouts or shots. He was driving through a stretch of desert country, with nobody in sight. Finally, though, he had had enough of the noises.

'You are getting too excited, Mr Fayne,' he said soothingly. 'But don't worry. This will calm you down!' He pressed the second button – the one which would start the knock-out gas streaming out from beneath the seats in the rear of the car.

There was a loud hissing noise. Fayne's shouts became fainter and fainter, the banging of his fists more and more feeble. And finally there was a total silence.

'Sweet dreams, Mr Fayne,' Stefan said into the mike, and did not stop chuckling to himself all the way to the secret headquarters.

Contact 33 was waiting on the pavement outside the entrance – a tall, grim-looking figure with thick lips and slanting eyes.

'You have brought Fayne?'

'Yes,' Kraski said. He was no longer chortling, being rather scared of Contact 33. 'He is in the back of the taxi, completely unconscious as you requested.'

'Good. You have done well, Kraski. Which is fortunate – because there would have been no mercy for you if you had bungled this. Open the door. I am anxious to see this brilliant British agent for myself.'

'Brilliant?' scoffed Stefan. 'He is no match for Stefan Kraski, sir, I can assure you. As a matter of fact, he struck me as being positively stupid!'

He pressed a button which unlocked the rear doors.

Contact 33 strode up to the taxi and opened

the nearest of them. He coughed and spluttered, and then reeled back as what was left of the knock-out gas struck him full in the face. But that was not the only thing that sent him reeling.

'You blundering fool!' he roared at Stefan. 'There's no one in your taxi at all! Maurice Fayne has completely disappeared.'

'Oh, no I haven't, old boy,' said a voice – and the tall, fair, crookedly-smiling figure of Maurice Fayne stepped out from behind the taxi.

'I'm far too interested in your new headquarters to do anything like that,' he went on. 'And now that I'm here, I'd be most grateful if you two gentlemen would show me round . . . After you've put your hands up, that is . . .'

Staring into the muzzle of Fayne's very deadly-looking gun, Stefan Kraski and Contact 33 had no choice but to put their hands high above their heads and do exactly what he said. They had the nasty feeling that it was *they*, not Maurice Fayne, who had walked into . . . the taxi trap.

Kraski's brain started whirling in a crazy spin. He had heard Fayne get into the car, and slam the door behind him. He had pressed a switch locking the doors, closing the windows, slamming shut the partition. He had heard Fayne banging on the doors and shouting, and even firing a revolver at the glass. He had switched on

the knock-out gas, and heard Fayne's shouting and banging weaken and then die away into silence. So how Fayne could possibly have turned up at the end of the trip, fully conscious, strolling out from behind the car, Kraski couldn't begin to think. Can you?

15 points if you can say how Maurice Fayne escaped from the taxi. 15 more points if you can explain everything that's puzzling Stefan in that last paragraph.

9

The Human Waxwork

Neville Lancaster, another man who prided himself on being just about the cleverest thief in the world, read the newspaper item again and again.

'PRICELESS RELIC GOES ON SHOW AT WAXWORKS MUSEUM.

'Mr Geoffrey Otis, proprietor of the Otis Waxworks Museum, Duke Street, London announced today that a jewelled dagger, dating from the time of the Civil War, will be on public display at his museum throughout the Christmas season.

'The dagger was recently discovered buried in a secret passage under Morton Towers, an old manor house in Shropshire. It is reckoned to have been buried there by some rich Cavalier while he was hiding from the Roundheads.

'"It's impossible to guess just how much the dagger would fetch at an auction," said Mr Otis, "but the jewels on it alone must be worth hundreds of thousands of pounds. It's a marvellous Christmas attraction for the museum. I'm displaying it in a proper historical setting. At each corner of the display stand there will be the waxwork figure of a Roundhead soldier, mounting guard with a pike.

' "Not that they'll be the only people guarding that dagger," he added with a grin. "There will be policemen on duty all the time, right outside the door. Even the cleverest thief in the world wouldn't have a hope of getting near it!" '

'Oh, he wouldn't, wouldn't he?' Neville Lancaster chuckled to himself as he put down the paper. 'We'll see about that, Mr Otis!'

The dagger, he read, was to go on display at the museum the following morning. He arrived there just after opening time and was, in fact, the first visitor of the day. He found that the dagger was being exhibited in a little room, not much bigger than a boxing ring. A notice just outside the door read: 'See the priceless relic for just £1!' An attendant was sitting underneath the notice waiting to take the £1 coins, and there was a uniformed policeman on duty beside him. But, Neville noticed, there was no one actually on guard inside the little room.

He gave the attendant £1 and walked in. The moment he did so, he saw the dagger. It was impossible to miss it. It was resting on a cushion in the centre of a big glass display case, with a powerful spotlight shining down on it so that its

jewelled hilt sparkled and shone with the daz-
zling force of a mirror reflecting the sun.

The four dummy Roundhead soldiers, one
standing at each of the four corners of the
cabinet, looked as though they'd turned their
backs in disgust on this showy Royalist trinket.

Neville took one glance at them – and started
violently. He could hardly believe his luck. One
of those four dummies – the one nearest the
door – was almost his own double! It had his
height, his build, his nose and even the same
colour eyes and hair.

That was when the great idea hit him. In the
days before he had been a criminal, Neville
Lancaster had been an actor. Not a very success-
ful actor, it was true. He'd only had walk-on
parts, and in one play, he had done nothing
except lie on the stage motionless for scene after
scene, pretending to be a corpse. That experi-
ence had done one thing for him, at any rate. It
had taught him how to keep still, without mov-
ing a muscle, for hour after hour.

If he could somehow sneak into the museum,
and take the place of that dummy –

He started making inquiries, and gradually a
master plan took shape.

The jewelled dagger, a chatty attendant told
him, was kept overnight in a safe in Mr Otis's
office. Every morning, just before the museum

opened, it was fetched out and put in the display cabinet in the exhibition room. Good, thought Neville. That meant that no one would be guarding the exhibition room before the dagger was put in there.

Next morning, he arrived at the museum long before opening time – in fact, before dawn. Once again, his luck was in. There was a window at the back of the little exhibition room, hidden behind a curtain, and it looked straight on to an alley at the side of the museum building. It was the easiest thing in the world to break open the catch and climb through into the room. Closing the window behind him, Neville set to work swiftly and silently.

Within a few seconds he had stripped the clothes off the dummy that was his double, and had dressed up in them himself. Everything fitted perfectly – the steel helmet, the breast-plate, even the doublet and hose. There was not even any need for a wig; the helmet covered most of his hair. (Roundheads wore their hair close-cropped – that's why they were called 'Roundheads'.)

There was one problem: where to hide the naked dummy. Looking round, Neville noticed that there was quite a lot of space under the display stand, and that it was covered by a convenient curtain. He stuffed the dummy in there, with his own discarded clothes piled neatly on top. Then he sat down, and ran over the rest of his master plan in his mind.

When the museum opened and the dagger was brought in, he'd be doing his waxwork act, standing as stiff as the other dummies, and holding a pike in front of him just as they did. Nobody would notice that there'd been any change. The exhibition room would open to the public as usual, and pretty soon, there'd be scores of visitors filing through the room, right past him. Then he would quietly drop a little gadget he'd brought with him to the floor. The moment it landed, it would explode with a blinding flash and fill the place with clouds of black smoke – smoke so thick that no one would see him as he smashed the glass of the cabinet, snatched the dagger and hid it under his uniform!

There would obviously be a moment of total panic and confusion. When the smoke cleared, the constables would be arresting and searching everyone . . . everyone except him, because, of course, by then he'd be back doing his dummy act again.

What happened next would depend on circumstances – but Neville imagined that the police would close the little exhibition room until the photographers and fingerprint men from Scotland Yard arrived. They obviously wouldn't stand guard over it. The jewelled dagger was gone, and that would be locking the stable door after the horse had bolted! It was any odds that he'd be left alone in the room – and it would take him only a few seconds to change back into his own clothes and dress up the dummy again. Then he'd slip behind the curtains and be away off through that window – leaving behind him one of the most baffling mysteries in the history of crime!

Neville was delighted with himself as he ran over these details in his head. It was a perfect plan. Nothing could possibly go wrong with it. There was no doubt about it – he *was* the

cleverest thief in the world, he told himself as, hearing footsteps approaching, he took up his position as a Roundhead waxwork.

A couple of seconds later an attendant brought the jewelled dagger into the room, followed by a policeman.

Less than two minutes later, Neville Lancaster found himself in handcuffs – because the policeman was very sharp-eyed, and had spotted three things that gave 'the cleverest thief in the world' away completely.

10 points for each of the three that you can spot. Mind you, you'll have to be pretty sharp-eyed yourself to do it!

10

The Dangerous Queen.

Of all the royal tyrants who terrorized Europe back in the dark days of the sixteenth century, one of the worst was Queen Eleanor of Brandavia.

Her rule was so brutal and vicious that, although revolutions were almost unheard-of in those times, the whole nation was suddenly on the brink of rebellion. The leader of the revolt was a reckless young man who called himself Peasant Waldo, and made the title sound as grand as though he had been Prince or Duke Waldo.

'And why should not a man take pride in being a peasant, if that is what God has made him?' he was heard to declare. 'I would a hundred times rather have the grubby, work-stained hands of a peasant than the bloodstained ones of our monstrous Queen!'

These words were high treason, of course. Not that that worried Peasant Waldo. A moment after he'd spoken them – in front of a large, cheering crowd in the market place of

Brandavia's capital city, Juro – he galloped off on his horse before any of the Queen's soldiers could catch him, and disappeared into his secret forest hideout.

Brandavia in those days was covered all over with forests, and finding an outlaw in one of them was almost impossible. Queen Eleanor sent search-parties of soldiers out in all directions – thousands of them, in what must have been one of the biggest manhunts in history. But a very strange thing happened. Out of those thousands of men, only hundreds returned. The rest, it was rumoured, had gone to join Peasant Waldo's rebel army.

Queen Eleanor began to be very frightened. It wasn't only soldiers who disappeared. Almost every day, some high-ranking person – a bishop, a general or even a duke – would disappear from her court, and again the rumours said that they had gone to join the rebels. The Queen suddenly realized that she didn't dare trust anybody, from her Lord Chamberlain down to her humblest scullery-maid. Any of them might prove to be a secret ally of the hated Waldo. There was nothing for it, she decided. She would have to deal with this insolent peasant herself, alone and unaided by anyone either in her court or on her palace staff.

It wasn't long before she'd hit on a cunning plan which would enable her to do just that – and rid her of this peasant pest for ever.

The next morning, she made the following announcement from her throne.

'We,' she said, meaning of course 'I', 'wish to issue an invitation to Waldo. If he really is as brave as his followers make out, let him come alone to my palace at the stroke of midnight tonight. The servants will let him in – but after that, they will retire to their quarters. Waldo has our royal promise that no one will lay hands on him. There will be no one *to* lay hands on him, for that matter – because we are ordering all soldiers, courtiers and even lords and ladies-in-waiting to leave the palace for the night. We desire the whole building to be deserted – except for Peasant Waldo and his Queen. Then, quite alone, unwatched and uninterrupted by a living soul, Waldo and we shall resolve our differences, and perhaps come to an agreement for what is nearest to our heart – the wellbeing and peace of all the people in the land.'

It was a bold speech, and left the courtiers stunned. Had this bloodthirsty tyrant Queen turned over a new leaf and decided to come to terms with her most bitter enemy?

The Lord Chancellor looked very nervous.

'Your Majesty,' he said. 'You are taking a fearsome risk. Peasant Waldo is a brilliant swordsman, and has no equal as a dagger-thrower. Insist at least that he is searched as he comes in – or he will have you at his mercy!'

Queen Eleanor laughed scornfully.

'I shall trust him,' she said. 'Even peasants have some ideas of chivalry. If he does not honour me as his Queen, at least I am sure he will not take advantage of a frail, defenceless woman . . . who wants only the happiness of all Brandavians, princes and peasants alike!'

At this show of courage, everyone at the court cheered and clapped. Her Majesty *had* changed, they thought. She had become a noble and fearless queen.

78

In fact, Eleanor was playing the most cunning and evil game of her life. The royal palace was a very old building, dating back to medieval times, and it contained a very sinister medieval device, known only to the Queen herself. The main room of the palace – the Throne Room – had a marble floor that was worked out in squares, almost like a huge chessboard. And one of those squares – as a matter of fact, the third from the left, three rows from the end – was in reality an *oubliette*. At the touch of a secret lever hidden under one of the arms of the throne, the square would open downwards like a trap door, and anyone who was standing on it would suddenly disappear from sight, to fall headlong down a deep pit, with a forest of spikes at the bottom.

The Queen's plan was as simple as it was cunning. She was sure that Peasant Waldo

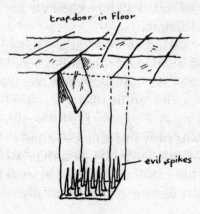

trap-door in Floor

evil spikes

would accept her offer. He was bound to do everything he could to help his fellow peasants. All she had to do was take him into the Throne Room, and get him walking round the floor while she talked from the throne. She would be full of flattery for his heroic deeds, so he would have no cause to reach for his sword or dagger. And sooner or later, he would be bound to step on that dangerous square. Then – at a touch of that lever – zwoosh! suddenly the rebel leader would be gone, never to be seen or heard of again. She would swear, of course, that he had left the palace, taking with him a secret treaty to show his followers. Was it her fault if some sad accident had befallen him before he returned to his forest retreat? Perhaps he hadn't had an accident. Perhaps he had been so moved by his face-to-face meeting with his Queen that he had repented of his wicked rebellion and fled the country in shame . . .

That was what she was going to say – and no one would be able to contradict her, because no one dreamt that the *oubliette* existed and so his body would never be found. It was a perfect plan!

There was only one thing she had to do before Peasant Waldo arrived, and that was to make sure that the *oubliette* was still in working order.

At about eleven o'clock that night, by which

time the whole palace was deserted on her own orders, Queen Eleanor went into the Throne Room. She had with her an old servant, who was carrying on his shoulders a heavy sack of chopped wood. 'Put that down exactly where we say, old Jaques,' the Queen commanded, 'and then go to your quarters and shut yourself in there for the night. Do you understand?'

Old Jaques nodded, and put the sack exactly where the Queen was pointing – on the third square from the left, third row from the end of the Throne Room.

'Right. Now leave us,' said the Queen.

When the servant's footsteps had died away, she climbed on to the throne, and sat for a moment looking at the sack. She wanted to be quite sure she remembered where that square was in the room. Then, taking a deep breath, she pressed the lever which was hidden under the left arm of the throne.

Nothing happened for a full three seconds, during which the Queen's blood ran cold. Then, from far beneath her, came a strange grinding creek – almost like a hollow groan. The square opened up and suddenly the sack was gone. There was a very, very long pause. Then came a distant, echoing *clang* as it landed heavily on the spikes far below. Finally the trap door shut again, leaving the marble floor looking just as it always did, with no sign of there ever having been a sack there at all.

The Queen laughed aloud. In an hour's time, what had happened to the sack would be happening to Peasant Waldo, she told herself. And she was still laughing an hour later, when she heard footsteps in the corridor. She just had time to put on a friendly, welcoming smile before Peasant Waldo came striding into the Throne Room.

Insolent peasant that he was, he didn't bow low when he saw her. He didn't even incline his head. He merely waved a hand and murmured:

'Good morrow, madam. I have heard tell that you wished me to come here alone tonight and talk with you. My friends,' he went on chattily, folding his arms, 'did not wish me to come. "We know the Queen," they said. "You will be walking into some cunning trap." "Trap or no trap," I told them, "never let it be said that I was too scared to come to any meeting that might help the peasants' cause." So here I am, madam, shaking like a leaf but determined to hear what words of wisdom you have to utter.'

Waldo didn't look as though he was shaking like a leaf. He was lounging against the wall as coolly as though he was watching a game of tennis or nine men's morris.

Queen Eleanor's blood boiled with fury. No

subject had ever before lounged about in her presence. A peasant like him should have fallen flat on his face at the sight of her, and started begging and praying for mercy. And she didn't at all like the way he was fingering his sword . . .

Just in time, she remembered that she had to be cunning – and that to be angry would spoil everything.

'Good morrow to you, friend Waldo,' she purred. 'At least I hope, sir, that from now onwards I will be able to call you friend.'

Waldo did not take his hand off the hilt of his sword.

'You have spared no efforts to hunt me down, and would no doubt far rather watch me dangling on the end of a rope than talk to me,' he said curtly. 'So why pretend that we are friends?'

The Queen managed – with great difficulty – a winning smile.

'I had not seen you then,' she said. 'I did not know you were so handsome or so brave, Peasant Waldo. Come closer, I beg you, and tell me what it is that you and your peasants want of me.'

To her relief, Waldo did come closer. He stepped forward three paces, which brought him to the third square from the left in the *second* row. If she could make him take just one more step forward . . .

'I think you know full well what the peasants want, Your Majesty,' he said coldly. 'It is to be free from your vicious, bloodthirsty rule.'

'You are actually asking me to abdicate – to give up my throne?'

Just for a moment, it was all Eleanor could do to keep calm. Her eyes blazed with murderous fury – and suddenly Waldo wasn't reaching for his sword, but for his dagger.

'I am afraid, madam, that nothing less would bring peace to this troubled realm,' he said.

With a great effort, Eleanor pulled herself together.

'In that case,' she said, 'I have something here that I believe you will be pleased to see.'

She picked up a document from a nearby table, and held it out to him. It was actually a proclamation offering 100 golden guineas for anyone who brought Waldo to the palace, dead or alive, but he wasn't to know that. She hoped he would think it was a promise to abdicate . . .

The trick worked – for a moment. Peasant Waldo stepped forward – but he was taking big strides now, which took him right past the dangerous square. And now he was striding right up to the throne.

'Stop!' she said desperately. 'It – it wasn't the document I thought it was . . .' She hurriedly put down the paper, and picked up a large bag instead. 'In any case, this will interest you more,' she shouted. 'There are hundreds of gold pieces here – enough to make you and all your peasant friends rich for life!'

Waldo was now right in front of her – on the third square from the left in the *fifth* row from the end of the room.

'Give them to me, I beg you,' he said. 'Not for my sake – but for the many peasant families I know who are close to starving.'

'In return for this – you will let me keep my throne?'

Waldo shook his head.

'By no means, dear lady. But when they hear of your kindness, my friends may let you keep – your life!' he said.

Eleanor laughed.

'Then the gold is yours, peasant – but you will have to grovel for it,' she said. And opening the bag, she sent the gold pieces rolling all over the floor. She was careful to see that some of them landed up in the third square from the left in the third row.

Waldo frowned.

'For myself, I would scorn to pick up a single piece,' he said. 'But this gold would mean so much to some of your poorest subjects, Your Majesty, that it is my duty to collect it for them.'

The next moment, he was stooping down and scooping up all the pieces on the square on which he was standing. A couple of seconds later, while a delighted Eleanor watched, he took a pace backwards and started on the ones that had fallen on the square just behind him. He was now, she reckoned, on the third square in the fouth row.

One more backward step would bring him to the dangerous square, thought the dangerous queen. And sure enough, two more seconds later, he took that fatal step – and must, she calculated, be right over the *oubliette*!

Shaking with a mixture of triumph, hate and

fury, Eleanor reached for the lever under the arm of the throne – and pressed it.

Nothing, she told herself, could save Peasant Waldo now.

Thirty points if you can spot what *can*.

11

The Clueless Clue-faker

'If it's the last thing I do,' Peggy Sullivan told herself over and over again, 'I'm going to get my own back on Fiona.'

Fiona Fradd had always been her deadly rival and enemy – right from the day they had both joined South Sidley High School a couple of years before. Mostly that was because Peggy was rather plain, with freckles all over her face, mousey brown hair that positively refused to curl, and a nose that obstinately turned up – while Fiona, with her large dark eyes and long hair, was attractive and glamourous and knew it. Knew it! She never let anyone forget it. She had once appeared in a television commercial for cornflakes, and still mentioned it at least a hundred times a day. What was more, she was the only girl in the class who used a grown-up perfume (Midnight Girl, by Renais of Paris, costing all of £8.50 for a microscopic bottle). She had a silver powder compact, too, given to her by her father, with FF engraved on its front – and she never stopped opening it up, and peering at herself in the little mirror inside its lid.

Peggy sat next to Fiona in Class 6A, and had been getting more and more irritated by her every day. But now things had got altogether beyond the joke. Peggy had become very attached to a boy called Roger Brown, who sat at the back of the class, and she was sure he was getting interested in her. They'd begun to exchange notes under the desks during the most boring lessons. But suddenly all that was over. Roger never replied to her notes now. He had eyes only for Fiona, and Peggy was sure that Fiona had deliberately enticed him away from her.

So that settled it. Somehow she *had* to get her revenge – and suddenly she hit on a plan. A plan that could end with nothing less than Fiona being expelled from the school!

The idea came to her during one of Mr Pendelbury's Maths lessons. Mr Pendelbury, the Assistant Head Teacher, was the only member of the staff who didn't seem to like Fiona. Throughout the lesson he kept shouting at her – once for not paying attention, once for giving a wrong answer, and once for getting out her compact and looking at herself in its mirror.

'Put that thing down immediately! How dare you bring it out during my lesson! You won't learn arithmetic by staring at your own stupid face, you bumptious, conceited child!' he roared.

Fiona put the compact down on her desk so fast that it might have been red-hot. Then, pulling out a small, pink handkerchief that wafted the aroma of Midnight Girl right round the room, she started dabbing her eyes, which were suddenly red and weepy.

'You've made her cry, Mr Pendelbury,' somebody said.

'Tough,' Mr Pendelbury replied. It was his favourite word.

Suddenly Fiona's eyes weren't red with crying. They were blazing with anger.

'Just you wait, Mr Pendelbury,' she said, under her breath.

That was when Peggy had her idea. Mr Pendelbury, being Assistant Head, had his own office – a small room just along the corridor from Class 6A. It had, Peggy remembered, a broken catch on the window, which meant that it could easily be opened from outside.

Supposing she sneaked back tonight, after school, and ransacked Mr Pendelbury's office? Everyone would naturally think that Fiona had done it . . . and to make absolutely *certain*, Peggy could leave fake clues all round the room. A handkerchief, for example, drenched in Midnight Girl perfume . . . Perhaps – perhaps even that famous compact –

Mr Pendelbury's lesson had been the last of the school day. Everyone in the class was getting ready to go home, except Fiona, who had already gone. She had stamped out in a fury, forgetting the compact, which was still lying where Mr Pendelbury had told her to put it, on her desk.

That was a stroke of luck if ever there was one, Peggy thought. Making sure that nobody was looking, she picked it up and slipped it into her satchel.

A moment later, she had another bit of luck. There was a bit of screwed-up paper lying on the floor under Fiona's desk. Opening it up, she read:

meet me at
8 p.m. outside
ssh!
Roger

So at 8 P.M. Fiona would be out somewhere on a hush-hush jaunt with Roger, would she? 'Ssh!' obviously meant that she wasn't to tell anyone where she was going. Which was great from Peggy's point of view. If she timed her raid on Mr Pendelbury's office for around 8 P.M., no one could say afterwards that Fiona was at home watching TV, or anything like that. Her enemy wouldn't have anyone to give her an alibi – except Roger himself, and who'd believe a boy friend?

So far, so very good, thought Peggy. But there were still a few problems. She'd wanted to leave a handkerchief smelling of Midnight Girl at the scene of the crime, but simply couldn't afford the £8.50 it cost for even the smallest bottle of the stuff. What was worse, in her family everybody used tissues, not handkerchiefs . . .

In the end, she solved both these problems fairly easily.

When she got home, she secretly searched the house and managed to find a handkerchief in the breast pocket of her father's best suit. Nipping out to the shops, she discovered a chemist's where small 'tester' bottles of perfume were on the counter, for customers to try free of charge. One of the perfumes featured was Midnight Girl.

Peggy snatched up the bottle, shook it all over her father's handkerchief, and managed to get out of the shop before a fist-waving assistant could stop her.

She still had one problem left. How was she going to sneak out of her own house at 8 P.M. without her parents spotting her? Then she remembered it was badminton night at the Youth Club she belonged to, when she was usually out anyway. So that difficulty melted into thin air.

She went off on her bike at the usual time, but instead of going to the club, pedalled swiftly down to the school. It was a black October night and the building was dark and deserted.

Peggy got off her bike, and tiptoed round to Mr Pendelbury's window. It opened easily, and the next moment she was inside the Assistant Head's office. She switched on the light. There

were curtains, but she didn't bother to draw them. No one ever came near the school building at night, she told herself.

Then she got busy. First she opened all the drawers of Mr Pendelbury's desk and threw their contents on to the floor. Next she yanked down all the pictures from the walls. Finally she went to a filing cabinet in the corner and tipped it over on its side with a crash.

She hadn't really done a great deal of damage – Peggy wasn't a vandal at heart – but she'd certainly done enough to get Fiona into a load of trouble. Now all she had to do was make sure it *was* Fiona who was blamed.

She took out the handkerchief reeking of Midnight Girl, and put it on the floor by the desk. Then she pulled the compact out of her satchel, holding it carefully by the edges. If the police were called in and took fingerprints, she wanted the only prints on that compact to be Fiona's!

Putting the compact carefully down on the floor on the other side of the desk from the handkerchief, she then set to work on her master-stroke. She took a large sheet of note-paper out of her satchel, and started to scrawl a message on it, in a close imitation of Fiona's handwriting. It was easy handwriting to copy, since Fiona always printed everything, like a book. She had to be careful about one thing, though. Fiona was the best girl at English in the class. It wouldn't do to make any silly grammatical mistakes. She wrote, slowly and carefully:

When she'd finished, she was very proud of her handiwork. When Mr Pendelbury saw it, he'd remember his last snort at Fiona – and start to suspect her straight away.

She checked very carefully to make sure she'd spelt 'Pendelbury' right. Then she remembered that there should be an apostrophe in 'isnt' and stuck one in, between the 's' and the 'n'.

Satisfied at last, she took a final look round the room – at the terrible mess she'd made and the three telltale clues pointing to Fiona: the handkerchief, the compact and the note. That should settle her enemy for good, she told herself and, chortling, she switched off the light and turned to the door.

In reality, she had nothing to chortle about at all. She had made at least four mistakes which showed clearly that it wasn't Fiona who had carried out the raid. And quite apart from that, she had missed a vital clue which should have warned her that she was almost certain to be found out.

As she discovered – the moment she opened the door and saw who was standing, waiting for her, right outside it!

There are five points for spotting each of Peggy's four mistakes . . . five more for saying what was the clue she'd missed . . . and a final five for saying who is standing outside that door.

12

The Nightmare Crime

WARNING NOTE. This final case is double-length, and contains a lot of red herrings (false clues). It has to be read really carefully if you want to spot the villain's mistake. He only makes one – but it's a very big one indeed . . .

Dr Aurelius Quarle was probably the most brilliant criminal in London during the 1930s – and the most unusual.

He was not only a very eminent Harley Street doctor; he was one of the most powerful hypnotists ever known. He had large black eyes, and the moment you stared into them you felt you were falling under his spell. He only had to bring out a pen or a pencil and wave it to and fro like a metronome in front of your eyes, and the next thing you knew you were nodding off into a trance. And when you came to, you could not remember anything about what had happened at all.

Dr Quarle frequently used his strange powers to heal people. Many a paralysed patient had

woken up from a trance able to walk again. Others with headaches and backaches and other kinds of pains had come to to find themselves completely cured.

But the good doctor was by no means always so good. In Harley Street he had a great many rich patients, and often, under these trances, he would ask them questions about where they kept their jewels. And he was such a brilliant hypnotist that he could get any sort of information out of them – including the combination numbers of their safes. He could even make them forget to close their windows or lock their doors . . . which made life very easy for him when at dead of night he set out, not as Dr Aurelius Quarle the master-hypnotist, but as Black Mask, the world's most wanted thief!

One day, Dr Quarle had a patient – a young lady called Mary Pilkington – who roused his interest. She was a rather pretty girl with fair hair and wide, almost baby-like blue eyes. It would be very easy to hypnotise her; he could tell that at a glance.

What he discovered about her interested him still more. She was, she told him, private secretary and personal assistant to Mr Belford Montague, the managing director of one of the best-known diamond merchants in Hatton Garden, London.

She had come to him because she had been suffering from bad headaches.

'I think I've been working too hard,' she said. 'Mr Montague gives me so much work to do that I'm at the office until eight o'clock nearly every night – long after everybody else on the staff has said goodnight and gone home.'

Dr Quarle raised his eyebrows.

'Mr Montague stays with you, dictating, I suppose?'

'Oh, good heavens no, not him. He says goodnight and goes off quicker than the rest! But he leaves me pages and pages of reports to type and letters to answer, so I just have to stay late to catch up.'

Dr Quarle's large black eyes started glowing.

'It doesn't seem right that a young woman like you should be left all alone in that office, night after night,' he said mildly. 'Supposing a thief broke in, after some of the firm's diamonds? Where are they kept, by the way?'

'In a big safe, in Mr Montague's office,' Miss Pilkington told him. 'But there's no need to worry. They'd never find it. It's hidden in a most unexpected place. I'm afraid I can't even tell *you*, doctor, where it is.'

'Of course not, my dear,' said Dr Quarle hastily. 'And of course, I wouldn't dream of asking. In any case, I imagine that even if a thief did know where the safe was, it wouldn't do him much good. No doubt it's very hard to break into.'

'Impossible, I'd say,' replied Miss Pilkington. 'It's solid steel. The walls are over a foot thick. It has a very tricky combination lock. You have to dial thirty-two digits! And *no one* knows the combination.'

'No one?' Dr Quarle looked quite startled. 'But surely, my dear Miss Pilkington, somebody must do. Otherwise, how can the safe ever be opened?'

Miss Pilkington burst out laughing.

'Mr Montague has a very, very clever scheme,' she said. 'He changes the combination every day. Then he tells it to me, and I scribble it down on a piece of paper. He doesn't remember it, once he's told it to me. I don't remember it, once I've written it down. Who *could* remember thirty-two digits? The only record of it is on that piece of paper, which I put in an envelope and then *post off to myself, to arrive the following morning!* It's a marvellous idea, don't you see?

'From the time I post that envelope in the afternoon, until it arrives back the following morning, nobody can possibly open the safe – because no one could crack a combination lock with thirty-two digits, and the number isn't known to anyone in the world! So no criminal could find it out – not even the cleverest jewel thief in London! Not even this Black Mask we're always reading about!'

Dr Quarle started slightly and his eyes gleamed dangerously. But they gave nothing away.

'Quite true, Miss Pilkington. It does look as if even Black Mask could never get the better of you and your brilliant employer. But that's enough chit-chat. Tell me about your headache.'

'It's terrible, doctor. I get it for hour after hour, day after day. Finally Mr Montague told me to take today off and come and see you. "And don't come back until the headache's completely gone, Mary," he told me, "even if it takes the rest of the week." If it does clear up, of course, I'll go back tomorrow. Not that I suppose there's the slightest chance of that, is there, doctor?'

Dr Quarle smiled.

'Stranger things have happened, my dear,' he told her gently. Then, bringing out his fountain pen, he began to swing it to and fro, to and fro, like a metronome.

'Just stare at this, Miss Pilkington . . . That's right – stare at it hard . . . It makes you feel very restful, doesn't it? Very . . . very restful . . . And that headache . . . it is simply floating away . . .'

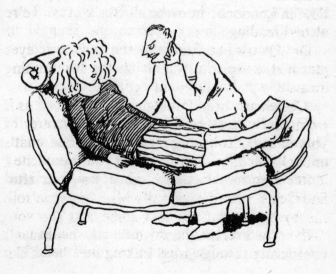

103

'That – that's right, doctor!' said an astonished Miss Pilkington. 'It really is floating away. Now – now it's gone.'

Dr Quarle smiled gently. He really was a very good doctor.

'Quite gone? You feel no pain at all?'

'No. None.'

'Excellent, Miss Pilkington. Now look at me.'

'At you, doctor?'

'Yes. Right into my eyes, please. Don't be afraid. I am not an ogre, I promise you. I have done something for you. Surely it isn't too much to ask you to do one little thing for me.'

'No . . . No . . . I suppose not . . .'

Miss Pilkington was feeling very sleepy now. She looked right into the doctor's eyes. They were like huge black saucers and seemed to swim towards her. Suddenly she had the feeling that it was she who was doing the swimming – that she was floating and nearly drowning in a vast black sea . . .

'Don't be frightened, my dear,' she heard Dr Quarle say. 'You are just having a little nightmare, which you will forget all about the moment you wake. Can you hear my voice loud and clear?'

'Y-yes, doctor.'

Every word that the doctor said was, in fact, thundering through Miss Pilkington's head like he roaring and crashing of a thousand waves: an irresistible force that had to be obeyed . . .

'Good. Now first I want you to give me a few facts. What is your office telephone number?'

She told him, and was vaguely aware that he grunted with satisfaction.

'Thank you,' he said. 'Now I want you to tell me something more important. You said that Mr Montague's safe was hidden in a most unexpected place. Just where is that place, please?'

There was a long pause. Even in her trance, Miss Pilkington hadn't forgotten that this information was highly secret.

But then Quarle's voice thundered through her head again, stern, commanding, and wiping out every other memory as easily as a flood tide sweeping bits of driftwood off a beach.

'I asked you a question, Miss Pilkington. I am waiting for the answer.'

'It's . . . it's in the little washroom leading out of the office,' she said. 'Dis – disguised as a washbasin stand. No one ever guesses it's there – because the taps on top of it really work. And so does the sink and everything . . .'

Dr Quarle was actually smiling now.

'Good. In fact, excellent,' he said. 'Now tell me this, Miss Pilkington. You are able to get into the washroom, I take it, even when Mr Montague has gone home?'

'Oh, yes. Both he and I have washroom keys.'

'Fine.'

Quarle slowly rose to his feet. His smile was broadening. He had thought out every detail of his master plan – a plan that would enable him to steal everything in Mr Montague's safe . . . And there would be jewels worth millions in there. This would be the biggest *coup* of Black Mask's career . . .

When he turned back to Miss Pilkington, his face was stern and commanding again. His eyes looked larger, darker, more terrifying than ever; and his voice sounded so powerful that every word seemed to make her start, as though it was sending an electric current through her.

'Listen very carefully, Miss Pilkington, to everything I say. And you will repeat every command I give you, to make sure that you have understood it. Right?'

'Y-yes, doctor.'

'Then tell me what I have just said.'

'I – I am to listen very carefully to everything you say, and repeat every command.'

'Good. Now in a few minutes I will count to three. When I say "three", you will wake up.'

'I will wake up.'

'You will not have the slightest sign of any headache.'

'I will not have the slightest sign of any headache.'

'And you will feel so fit that you will ring up Mr Montague and tell him you want to return to work first thing tomorrow.'

'First . . . thing . . . tomorrow . . .'

'You will not remember anything about this interview, of course. And tomorrow you will go through a normal working day. Except for one thing.'

'Except . . . for . . . one . . . thing . . .'

'When Mr Montague changes the combination of the safe, and asks you to write it down, you will memorize every digit. Those numbers will burn themselves into your brain as though they were written in fire. Do you understand?'

'I . . . understand . . .'

'Then tomorrow night, you will do as you always do. You will stay alone in the office, working late. Even if Mr Montague does not give you so much work, you will still find some excuse to do that. Right?'

'Yes. I will stay alone . . . working late . . .'

'That's right. In other words, you will carry on as usual – until and unless you hear a certain codeword which I will teach you. As soon as you hear that codeword, you will go into a trance.'

'I will go into – a trance.'

'You will walk straight into the washroom, and using the combination you have memorized, you will open the safe.'

'I will open the safe.'

'You will take out everything it contains – diamonds, bank notes, bonds, everything – and put them in a sack. Then you will return to your desk and wait there, with the sack in front of you, until you hear a knock on the front door of the office. When you hear the knock you will come downstairs, carrying the sack, and will hand it to whoever is at the door.'

'I will take out everything the safe contains – '

While Miss Pilkington duly repeated everything he had said, Dr Quarle was suddenly almost beside himself with excitement. He couldn't help pacing round and round, up and

down the room. In just over twenty-four hours, he'd have a fortune in his grasp!

There was just one more thing left to do. And that was to make up a good code word – the word which, the moment she heard it, would send her back into a trance and make her his willing slave.

Suddenly he thought of the perfect word: one that would remind her instantly of all she'd been through.

'NIGHTMARE!' he said aloud. 'That is the codeword, Miss Pilkington. As soon as you hear it, you will instantly proceed to carry out all these instructions. Say it after me, three times, just to make sure you've got it into your head.'

'Nightmare,' said Miss Pilkington dully. 'Nightmare, nightmare . . .'

'Good.' Aurelius Quarle stopped pacing, and came and stood over her. His voice was no longer stern; it was just a soft, coaxing whisper in her ear.

'Right, then. At the count of three, you will wake up, and remember nothing about all this until you hear that word . . . one . . . two . . . THREE!'

Miss Pilkington blinked twice, and sat up.

'Where am I?'

'In my consulting-room, Miss Pilkington. You have just had a little snooze, that's all. How's your headache?'

'Headache?' Miss Pilkington suddenly smiled all over her face. 'Why, it's completely gone! Thank you so much, Doctor. You're a miracle worker! I feel so well that I could go back to the office tomorrow!' An idea seemed to come to her out of the blue. 'In fact, that's what I'll do. I'll ring Mr Montague and tell him I'll be back – first thing tomorrow . . .'

Dr Quarle was smiling all over *his* face when he showed her out. Tomorrow, he told himself, was going to be the most triumphant day of his – or rather, Black Mask's – career!

At 7 P.M. the following evening, he drove round to Hatton Garden, and went straight into a telephone kiosk opposite the office of Montague & Co. He could see a light on in one of the office windows. Good, he thought. Miss Pilkington was working late. Only one window was lit up; obviously she was on her own as usual. He picked up the phone and dialled her office number.

'Montague & Company,' he heard her say in a dazed, dull voice. 'Mary Pilkington speaking.'

He pressed the button in the call box – Button A it was called in those days – which enabled him to reply. He said just one word, very softly but with magnetic force.

'NIGHTMARE.'

Miss Pilkington said nothing. She just replaced her receiver with a faint 'click'.

Dr Quarle smiled his satisfaction. That was just what she would do if she'd gone into her trance. Now, doubtless, she was walking away from the phone, straight into the washroom where –

He slipped out of the phone box, returned to his car, and waited there for another ten minutes. That would be plenty of time, he reckoned, for Miss Pilkington to open the safe and transfer its contents to a sack. What would those contents be? He visualized diamonds by the dozen, each wrapped in a delicate velvet bag

. . . money, too – perhaps hundreds of thousands of pounds in notes . . .

He was out of the car now, and a few seconds later was knocking on the door of Montague & Co's offices. It was dark in the doorway. No one passing along Hatton Garden could see him as he slipped on his famous black mask. It would be the last time he would ever have to wear it, he told himself. He should be able to make enough tonight to retire from crime for ever.

He heard footsteps behind the doors. They were light, sharp, robot-like footsteps. Miss Pilkington, of course, walking in a trance, he told himself.

Then the door opened. Sure enough, it *was* Miss Pilkington, with a heavy-looking sack in her hands.

Dr Quarle felt a sense of triumph flooding through him . . . but the feeling didn't last long. Only, in fact, until Mr Montague himself stepped out from behind the door, accompanied by a Chief Detective Inspector from Scotland Yard who immediately slapped handcuffs on Dr Quarle and said:

'Hypnotize your way out of them, sir, if you can!'

Aurelius Quarle's black eyes blazed behind the slits of his black mask – but not with hypnotic intensity. He was too busy trying to

work out just where the most brilliant scheme of his career had gone wrong. Thirty points if you can beat him to it.

Solutions
or, Mistakes Unlimited!

1: *The Monster Mistake*
The party was on Saturday, October 31 – so the next morning was a Sunday, when holding up banks is just a little difficult, because none of them happen to be open.

2: *The Treasure Hunt Cheat*
East is East and West is West, as the old poem goes. But not on Bertie Binn's map, where East is West, and West is East. No wonder he wound up on the Head's flowerbed.

3: *The Boy Who Was Caught Red-Handed*
It wasn't only the curly letters that made David Greyfield's writing pretty weird. He also wrote every word slanting a different way – the first word slanting to the right, the second to the left and so on. He managed to get all the curls out of his letters when he wrote the note – but never thought about straightening the letters themselves. No doubt it won't take long for Cilla to straighten him out . . .

4: *The Master Disguiser*

The second time he disguised himself, the MD forgot about the tinted contact lenses – and so his eyes were now his own natural grey instead of the piercing Kilberkoff blue that they had been the day before. Quite enough to make any astute bank manager look at the situation with – er – different eyes!

5: *The Perfect Theft*

1. Ferdinand has forgotten to take off those black rubber gloves, and is slipping out of the study into the drawing room still wearing them! They are not exactly the corret wear for smart West End parties, and if anyone sees him with them, or slipping them into his pockets, they're going to ask some very awkward questions.

2. Even if Ferdinand pockets the gloves without being seen, he's still not out of trouble. The next time she goes into the study, Mrs Denton will see at a glance that someone has been at the safe because, although he replaced all the other items in order, in the darkness he *completely forgot about the willow pattern plate* – the most important ornament of the lot, because it actually hid the safe!

3. You might say that even if the robbery is spotted, there's still nothing to point to Ferdinand being the thief. (As long as nobody spotted

those gloves, that is.) But the first thing the police are going to do is examine the fake diamond – and Ferdinand has left his fingerprints all over that, because, if you remember, he examined it *before* putting on those gloves!

6: *The Destroyer of Planet Earth*

There is 'one big difference between Donyxians and human beings' which 'can be concealed if they take enough care'. But this big difference makes it painful to sit in the driver's seat of a car (Clue 1) and very painful to wear a seat belt (Clue 2). This means that it is probably something that you sit on. It is also something the sight of which makes the attendant turn white when he gets a rear view of Zavaldo, after Zavaldo's suit had been ripped open down the back (Clue 3). From these three clues, it should be possible to guess that Donyxians have monkey-like *tails*, which they fold up and conceal with difficulty beneath their suits.

As he made his headlong dash down the corridor to the caves, Zavaldo's tail must have broken through his suit entirely, and tagged along behind him. It was obviously quite a long tail too – long enough for a policeman to grab it at three paces' distance, and pull on it so painfully that the Donyxian dropped first the briefcase and then the ray-gun.

If you think this is a tall story, remember, some scientists reckon that *we* have the remains of tails in our bodies. If we'd been born on another planet . . .

7: *The Gliding Ghost*

1. Because it's in pitch darkness and she's broken her torch, Celia has never had a chance to see along the path behind the wall. So how can she be sure that the sloping bit (see the view from the classroom window) isn't, in fact, a flight of downward steps? Roller-skating along the path in the dark, she would be likely to pitch headlong down those steps – and the gliding ghost would be flying, probably over the wall to land at Miss Frenais' feet!

2. If Miss Frenais made an 'r' noise at the back of her throat when she pronounced 'Abbé Huge', it is obvious that she was really saying 'Abbé Rouge'. And *rouge* – one of the very first

words which everyone learns in French – means, of course, red. Only Celia, the dimmest girl at French in the school, would use a green coat and hood for the ghost of the Red Abbot!

8: *The Taxi Trap*

Maurice Fayne had realized the moment he saw Stefan Kraski's taxi that it was probably a trap. But he thought it might lead him to the enemy's secret HQ. So he decided to get in, making silly remarks as he did so, to make Kraski think he was an idiot.

He didn't stay in the taxi long, though – in fact, not more than a few seconds. Before Kraski had pressed the button locking the doors and closing the windows, he had climbed out again – through the opposite door.

Then he hung on to the *outside of the car* for the rest of the trip, like this:

There were no passers-by to notice him, because most of the journey, remember, was through a desert wasteland. And to make sure that Kraski didn't suspect what had happened, he made banging noises on the door, shouted 'Help! Let me out!' and even fired off his revolver. He kept quiet, of course, once he heard the sound of hissing gas inside the car.

When the taxi drove up outside the HQ, it was a simple matter to jump off and run behind it before Kraski or Contact 33 could see him. Then he was all set to spring his own 'taxi trap'!

9: *The Human Waxwork*

If you look again at the picture of the four waxwork dummies, and then compare it with the picture of Neville posing as a dummy, you'll see Neville's big mistakes. Three of the dummies are holding their pikes upright, but the dummy

closest to the door is different: its pike has slipped into a sloping position. And Neville, remember, is supposed to be taking the place of that dummy by the door!

There's another way in which that 'door dummy' differs from the others – it has a slight Cromwellian moustache, whereas Neville is clean-shaven.

And the third mistake? Neville hid the wax-work, with his own clothes piled on top, under the display cabinet. He thought they would be hidden by the curtain there. But as you can see from the first picture, the curtain stops a good few inches above the floor. And if you look closely enough at the picture of Neville in his dummy get-up (p. 73) you'll just be able to see one of the dummy's eyes staring out from under the curtain – almost as though it was trying to give the policeman the wink!

10: *The Dangerous Queen*

Yes, Peasant Waldo *is* on the dangerous square, and the trapdoor *is* about to open beneath him. But it won't happen for three seconds (that's the time it takes for the mechanism to work – as we discovered when the sack went down). And after every two seconds, Waldo moves on to another square. So he should be stepping off the dangerous square with a second to spare!

Mind you, he'll be pretty angry . . . and if you want to know the end of the story, he brings out his sword and forces the tyrant queen to write and sign an abdication on the spot. There's no one to stop him, because everyone's been ordered by the Queen herself to keep away!

11: *The Clueless Clue-Faker*

Peggy made so many mistakes that you may well have spotted a few that I haven't. But her four worst ones were:

1 Fiona, being a glamorous type, uses small, pink handkerchiefs. The one from Peggy's father's breast-pocket would be a big white one – men's size. A very unlikely thing indeed for

Fiona to carry around with her, let alone be careless enough to drop at the scene of the crime!

2 Peggy was right about the 'isnt' in that note

needing an apostrophe – but it should go between the 'n' and the 't', not the 's' and the 'n'.

3 A girl good at English would have realized that the 'its' should have an apostrophe too – between the 't' and the 's'.

4 And what's the good of carefully leaving Fiona's fingerprints on the compact when you're leaving your own fingerprints all over the room? There's no mention of Peggy wearing gloves – and as you can see from the hands in the picture, she's definitely not wearing any when writing that note. (Fingerprints show up on notepaper better than almost anywhere.)

Finally, the clue that Peggy should have spotted was in Roger's message to Fiona. '*Meet you at 8 p.m. outside – SSH!*' was how she read it, but that doesn't really make a lot of sense. It's far more likely that the message meant '*Meet you at 8 p.m. outside SSH*' with the 'SSH' standing for South Sidley High! In other words, Roger and Fiona were meeting at 8 p.m. right outside the school building. They could hardly have helped seeing Peggy go in and, of course, they crept up and watched everything she did. (She'd turned on the light but hadn't bothered to draw the curtains.) So obviously, it was Roger and Fiona who were waiting to have a few words with her the moment she got outside the door.

12: *The Nightmare Crime*

Dr Quarle has told Miss Pilkington to carry on with her normal working day until or unless she hears the codeword 'Nightmare'. But the moment she does hear it, she is to go straight into a trance, head for the hidden safe, and start to load its contents into a sack.

Which is fine – as long as she doesn't hear the word until she is alone in the office, working late. What Dr Quarle has failed to realize is that she is, in fact, bound to hear that word very much earlier!

We know that her boss, Mr Montague, calls her 'Mary'. (At one point, she quotes him as saying 'Take a day off – and don't come back until the headache's gone, Mary.') We also know that he says goodnight to her before he goes home.

The odds, then, are about a million to one that this evening, just before he left, he said: 'Good *night, Mary*' – whereupon, to his astonishment, he would have seen her go into an instant trance and start rifling his secret safe before his eyes! (Note: When Quarle rang Mary up and said, 'Nightmare,' the word had no effect because, of course, she was already in a trance – as he might have guessed from her 'dazed, dull voice'.)

Mr Montague was obviously a pretty bright

man. (Managing Directors of diamond merchants usually are.) He put two and two together, and realized what was happening. He didn't try to wake Mary out of her trance; he just called up a Chief Detective Inspector whom he knew. He and the Inspector just watched and waited until Mary heard the knock on the door and went to answer it, with the sack in her arms. Then they pounced, and the most brilliant criminal in London was (go on, say it with me this time) FOILED AGAIN . . .